SYNAESTHESIA

tasting words
in a rainbow of sound

Sue Johnson

TOADSTONE PRESS

SYNAESTHESIA: tasting words in a rainbow of sound

DEDICATION

To artist and writer Jenny Gunn – thank you for changing my view of the world.

DEFINITION

A condition in which one type of stimulation evokes the sensation of another, as when the hearing of music produces the visualisation of colour.

The UK Synaesthesia Association gives the following description:

In its simplest form it is best described as a "union of the senses" whereby two or more of the five senses that are normally experienced separately are involuntarily and automatically joined together. Some synaesthetes experience colour when they hear sounds or read words. Others experience tastes, smells, shapes or touches in almost any combination. These sensations are automatic and cannot be turned on or off. Synaesthesia isn't a disease or illness and is not at all harmful. In fact, the vast majority of synaesthetes couldn't imagine life without it.

SYNAESTHESIA

tasting words
in a rainbow of sound

Sue Johnson

TOADSTONE PRESS

CONTENTS

INTRODUCTION

Imagine when you see a city skyline you taste blackberries. Or when you hear a violin you get a tickle on your left knee. Maybe Saturday is indigo blue…

Synaesthesia is a neurological condition in which two or more of the five senses normally experienced separately are involuntarily joined together. When the brain is examined under clinical conditions, stimulation in one area will cause a different part of the brain to respond too.

It is thought that babies are born with the sensory synapses fused, so that they experience life in a bit of a muddle. By the age of four, the synapses separate – apart from approximately 4% of the population where one or more sense will remain linked to another.

There are up to 70 different types of synaesthesia with the most common varieties involving colour. One person describes her back pain as lavender squiggles, another person thinks chicken tastes spherical. Some synaesthetes experience colour when they hear sounds or read words. Others experience tastes, smells or shapes.

Many people with synaesthesia experience the letters of the alphabet or the days of the week as a specific colour. Sometimes this will appear in their mind's eye – other people see the colours appear in front of them. Every synaesthete has their own colour palette. One lady I met said Fridays were pillar-box red. A man said they were definitely emerald green.

For some people, the months of the year may appear in a specific place. For instance, July may be behind them whereas November is above their head.

Many instances of synaesthesia relate to the links between colour and sound or colour and shape – for example the way that Kandinsky painted the music he heard or the way that Liszt saw music as specific colours.

I have lexical-gustatory synaesthesia where some names and words have a specific taste. These are mainly words or names I experienced prior to the age of about four. The taste has no relation to what the word represents. It also involves no conscious thought on my part – the impulse comes from my brain not my mouth and has nothing to do with imagination. Some people who try to apply logic to the condition find the idea impossible to grasp. One man argued with me and said that 'feather' couldn't possibly taste of whipped cream. It would have to be something crunchier!

The tastes I experience have not changed, even though they may relate to food I haven't actually eaten since I was three. The taste is clear and unchanged by time.

In this short book, I have tried to give an explanation about synaesthesia for people who are not scientists.

It is something I feel very privileged to have been given.

Further information about my poetry, stories and novels can be found at www.writers-toolkit.co.uk

HISTORY

The scientific world has known about synaesthesia for three centuries – but it keeps forgetting that it knows!

The first reference to synaesthesia historically was in 550 BC when Pythagoras developed mathematical equations for musical scales. He said that musical notes could be seen as "relationships between numbers."

In 370 BC Plato wrote to Timaeus that the sound of the world had the same musical ratios as those suggested by Pythagoras – "the music of the spheres."

Reference is made to a possible synaesthetic reaction in the Bible. In Exodus Chapter 20 Verse 18, Moses comes down Mount Sinai with the Ten Commandments: "And all the people saw the voices. And all the people heard the visions."

The link between sound and colour continued to be explored across the centuries. In the 1700s, the French Jesuit monk Louis Bertrand Castel created his *clavecin des couleurs* with the aim of making sound visible.

In 1739, Lorenz Christoph Mizler created his "schema for coloured notes." This was:

A   Indigo
B   Violet
C   Red
D   Orange
E   Yellow
F   Green
G   Blue

Anyone who has studied yoga will know that these colours and notes, in this order, correspond to those relating to the energy centres in the body called chakras. This begins with Red at the base chakra (just below the tail bone) (Note C) and moving up the body to the crown of the head. (Note B).

Many people have reported successful healing with colour and sound therapy.

The first documented case of synaesthesia was by Georg Tobias Ludwig Sachs in 1812. He published a medical dissertation that described himself, his albinism and his synaesthesia.

He describes his synaesthesia in the third person by saying: "I cannot express it better than to say that a coloured idea appears to him… particularly those things that form a simple series – e.g. numbers, the days of the week and letters of the alphabet…"

He continues by describing how zero appears "as if it were very light and bright in a pale yellow colour, while the number four is vermillion, six is indigo…"

In the mid nineteenth century, the French symbolist writers Rimbaud and Baudelaire wrote poems which focused on synaesthetic experiences. Neither of them were true synaesthetes. The effects they experienced were achieved by the use of drugs.
In 1857, Charles Baudelaire wrote 'Correspondences' which did much to popularise literary synaesthesia.

Here is an extract from it:

"Nature is a temple whose living colonnades
Breathe forth a mystic speech in fitful sighs.
Man wanders among the symbols in those glades
Where all things watch him with familiar eyes.

Like dwindling echoes gathered far away
Into a deep and thronging unison
Huge as the night or as the light of day,
All scents and sounds and colours meet as one.

Perfumes there are as sweet as the oboe's sound,

Green as the prairies, fresh as a child's caress,
-    And there are others, rich, corrupt, profound

And an infinite pervasiveness,
Like myrrh, or musk, or amber, that excite
The ecstasies of sense, the soul's delight."

In 1872, Arthur Rimbaud wrote a poem about coloured vowels
entitled 'Voyelles.'

"A black E white I red
U green O blue: vowels
I will one day declare
your latent births:
A, black velvet corset
of exploding flies
which buzz around cruel stenches
Gulfs of shadow
E, candours of vapours and tents
lances of proud glaciers
white kings shivering umbels."

Research on synaesthesia was also carried out by Sir Francis Galton
– a cousin of Charles Darwin.

This inspired further work by de Rochas, Lauret and Abertoni.

Interest in synaesthesia peaked between 1860 and 1930 and then it
was forgotten – possibly because psychology and neurology were
premature sciences at that time. Behaviourism took over and
subjective experience like synaesthesia was deemed not a proper
subject for scientific study. It was never mentioned or acknowledged
when I was a child and young adult.

In the 1980s, a revival in interest took place – possibly because body scanning equipment was now available.

Scientist Richard Cytowic met a man at a dinner party who was making a sauce and couldn't get it to taste right. He kept saying 'it needed more points in it.'
This led to Cytowic undertaking further research and writing a book called 'The Man Who Tasted Shapes.'

His criteria for synaesthesia are:

1.   It is involuntary and automatic.
2.   Synaesthetic images are spatially extended.
3.   Synaesthetic perceptions are constant and generic.
4.   Synaesthesia is highly memorable.
5.   Synaesthesia is laden with affect.

In 1987, Simon Baron-Cohen, researching at Cambridge University, found the first hard evidence that synaesthetes' experiences are measurable in the brain and constant across time.

HEREDITY

Synaesthesia runs in families, although it may skip a generation and may not affect immediate relatives.

It is possible for only one twin to have the condition. Some people outgrow it or claim that the sensations are less vivid as they get older.

In terms of genetics, a mother can pass on the condition to a son or a daughter. A father can only pass it on to a daughter via the X chromosome. It is inherited as an X linked dominant trait. A significant number of people with synaesthesia are left-handed.

Women synaesthetes predominate – in the US in 1989 Cytowic found a ratio of 3:1 while in the UK Baron-Cohen found a ratio of 8:1 in 1993.

There is evidence to suggest that synaesthesia may be linked to dyslexia, autism and attention deficit disorder. (My brother and his three daughters are dyslexic.)

THE LINK BETWEEN SYNAESTHESIA AND AUTISM

Autism is diagnosed when a person struggles with social relationships and communication and shows unusually narrow interests and resistance to change.
Autism is said to involve over-connectivity of neurons so that the person over-focuses on small details but finds it hard to keep track of the big picture.

On the face of it, it doesn't look like a pairing. Synaesthesia involves atypical connections between areas of the brain not usually wired together so that a sensation in one area automatically triggers a perception in another.

Research by scientists at Cambridge University suggests that 18.9% of people diagnosed with autism have some form of synaesthesia – with the most common variety being grapheme-colour. (See page 10.)

This is thought to have major implications for educators designing autism-friendly learning environments. The national supermarket chain Morrison's has been in the news recently because they are planning to introduce 'Autism Hour' – a quiet hour when noise, lighting and crowds are limited in order to reduce sensory overload.

CAN YOU ACQUIRE SYNAESTHESIA?

Synaesthesia-like symptoms can be experienced after taking hallucinogenic drugs such as LSD or magic mushrooms. (Charles Baudelaire and Arthur Rimbaud created work as a result of such experiments in the 19th century).

Hypnosis, head massage and meditation can also give some people temporary synaesthetic reactions.

Some medication prescribed for mental health conditions – e.g. bipolar – can give synaesthesia-like side-effects.

It can also develop as a result of sensory loss – e.g. stroke, blindness or deafness.

TYPES OF SYNAESTHESIA

The most common varieties relate to colour. Non-synaesthetes will often agree that the colour blue elicits a 'cool' sensation while orange and red are 'hot.'

Grapheme-Colour Synaesthesia

This is the most common form of synaesthesia. Individual letters of the alphabet and numbers are collectively called 'graphemes.' So, for people with grapheme-colour synaesthesia, these individual letters of the alphabet and numbers each have an assigned, perceived colour that does not change over time.

Lexical-Gustatory Synaesthesia

This is one of the rarest forms of synaesthesia, in which people have associations between words and tastes. It is experienced by less than 0.2% of the population. (This is the variety that I have.) The only other person I have met with this type of synaesthesia is James Wannerton, Chairman of the UK Synaesthesia Association. He reported that his nephew is toffee flavoured, his granny tastes of condensed milk and his next door neighbours are a mixture of 'yogurt, jelly beans and a subtle hint of a waxy substance.'

Mirror-Touch Synaesthesia

Imagine you watch someone reach up and touch their own chin, but that you experience a touch on your own chin. This is mirror-touch synaesthesia – when you feel the same sensation another person feels. Even amongst non-synaesthetes, around 30% of people have a mild form of this in that they experience pain when they see someone else being hurt. It is thought that this may be a heightened version or part of the process involved in how we empathise with others.

Misphonia

While many forms of synaesthesia are harmless and some consider it enhances their life, not all forms are beneficial. Misophonia – literally 'hatred of sound' – is a condition in which sounds trigger strong negative emotions like disgust and anger. It's extremely rare and may be caused by problematic connections between the auditory cortex and the limbic system. Commonly reported amongst misophones are strong adverse feelings in response to the sounds of other people eating and breathing.

Ordinal-Linguistic Personification
This is where ordered sequences like numbers, days of the week or letters all have particular personalities, and even appearances. Monday might be a lively young girl in a red dress whereas Tuesday might be an old woman with grey hair and a shopping basket.

Number-Form Synaesthesia
This was documented by Sir Francis Galton over a century ago. Numbers automatically appear in the mind as mental maps. The areas of the brain for processing numbers and for spatial representations are relatively close to each other, but every synaesthete will have their own idea of what their map looks like.

Chromosthesia
This is sound to colour synaesthesia. When people with chromosthesia hear sounds it will automatically and unintentionally make them experience colours. (Some non-synaesthetes will know what it's like to hear a particular song that reminds them of a place they used to live). Some synaesthetes will see the colours projected into a space in front of them, others will see it in their mind's eye. Some may experience it on hearing the spoken word – for example a railway station announcement.

Olfactory-Visual
This is where a smell will evoke a colour. The colour may have no bearing on what the item is. For instance, the smell of coffee may evoke the colour green, whereas the smell of bread baking is a buttercup yellow.

There are obviously many more types – for further information, see some of the websites listed at the end of this book.

CHARACTERISTICS OF PEOPLE WITH SYNAESTHESIA

Intelligent

Left handed/ambidextrous

Confuse left and right

Poor sense of direction

Good memory

Possibility of depression

Hypersensitive

Hate crowds

Nocturnal

Prone to migraine

Solitary

Poor at maths

Creative – music/art/poetry

Prone to déjà vu, clairvoyance, vivid dreams

Open to paranormal experiences

Most of these are certainly true for me – although I'm not sure about the intelligence bit! It depended on which teacher you were asking!

I am left-handed/ambidextrous.

I nearly always confuse left and right and turn the wrong way when coming out of shops etc. I cannot read a map!

I do have an excellent memory and recall events clearly from a very early age (less than one year old).

I have had bouts of mild depression/anxiety, including post-natal depression with one of my daughters, but nothing that has ever needed medication or treatment.

I am hypersensitive and can pick up on an atmosphere or person not being right very quickly.

I don't like crowds – and prefer to be on the end of a row in a cinema rather than in the middle.

I am often awake during the night reading and writing.

I don't get migraines (or any sort of headache) and although I like my own company I also love being with other people.

I was poor at maths at school – which is strange because most of my father's family were in banking. However I missed a lot of the early stages due to illness and never really caught up in the school system. Consequently, it depended on the subject of the lesson as to whether I was classified as 'outstanding' or 'dim.'

I have written stories ever since I could write! I also enjoy artwork and writing guitar tunes.

I have seen ghosts on several occasions. I am also quick to pick up on 'cold spots' and atmospheres in various places. I have vivid dreams that become stories, poems and scenes from novels. I also experience déjà vu on occasions.

I suspect my mother's sister may have had some form of synaesthesia. She was certainly on the autistic spectrum and could remember every meal she'd eaten on the holidays she'd had in various parts of the UK – including what she was wearing at the time.

My father had an unusually vivid imagination and was a brilliant storyteller. He also saw ghosts on several occasions.

FAMOUS PEOPLE WITH SYNAESTHESIA

Synaesthesia is said to be eight times more common amongst writers, artists, musicians and other creative people.

Duke Ellington
He described the notes in music in terms of colour and texture. To him, the D Major chord was dark blue burlap, whereas G Major was light blue satin.

F Scott Fitzgerald
He referred to the "yellow cocktail music" played during the 1920s.

Joanne Harris
One of my favourite authors, Joanne Harris, has olfactory-visual synaesthesia where she experiences colours as scents. She says that red smells like chocolate. This is the reason why, in her novel *Chocolat,* that Vianne and her daughter are often surrounded by the colour red.

Jimi Hendrix
He described chords and harmonies in terms of colour. He declared that the chord E7#9 was "the purple chord" and used it to help form the verse for his song 'Purple Haze.' (This is often referred to by guitarists as "the Hendrix chord.")

Billy Joel
"I would say the softer more intimate songs, there's 'Lullaby,' 'And so it goes,' 'Vienna' and another called 'Summer, Highland Falls' – when I think of melodies that are slower or softer, I think in terms of blues or greens. When I (see) a particularly vivid colour, it is usually a strong melodic, strong rhythmic pattern that emerges at the same time. When I think of these songs I think of vivid reds, oranges and golds. (From an interview with Maureen Seaberg).

Wassily Kandinsky
His 1911 painting 'Impression III' was inspired by Schoenberg's music at a concert in Munich. He said: "The vivid wash of yellow

describes the sound itself. Colour is the keyboard. The eye is the hammer. The soul is the piano with its many strings. The artist is the hand that purposely sets the soul vibrating by means of this or that key."

Franz Liszt

When Liszt first began as Kapellmeister in Weimar in 1842 it astonished the orchestra that he said: "Oh please, gentlemen, a little bluer if you please! This tone type requires it." Or: "That is a deep violet, please, depend on it! Not so rose!"

At first the orchestra thought he was joking, but as time went on, they got used to the fact that the great musician genuinely seemed to see colours.

Marilyn Monroe

In Norman Mailer's biography of Marilyn Monroe, he states that: "She has a displacement of the senses that others take drugs to find."

Her second husband Joe Di Maggio claimed that she couldn't cook. Marilyn often dished up a plateful of carrots and peas "because she liked the colours."

Wolfgang Amadeus Mozart

He said that the key of D Major had a warm "orangey" sound to it. B Flat Minor was blackish, whereas A Major was a rainbow of colours. It may explain why he used different colours when writing some of his musical notes and why a lot of his music focuses on the major keys.

Edvard Munch

When writing about his famous painting *The Scream,* he wrote:

"I was walking along a path with two friends – the sun was setting – suddenly the sky turned blood red. I paused, feeling exhausted and leaned on the fence. There was blood and tongues of fire above the blue-black fjord and the city. My friends walked on and I stood there trembling with anxiety – and I sensed an infinite scream passing through nature."

Vladimir Nabokov

In his autobiography 'Speak Memory' published in 1966, the author of 'Lolita' writes about his fine case of coloured hearing. "Perhaps hearing is not quite accurate since the colour sensation seems to be produced by the very act of my orally forming a letter while I imagine its outline. The long 'A' of the English alphabet (and it is this alphabet I live on unless otherwise stated) has for me the tint of weathered wood, but a French 'A' evokes polished ebony. The black greys also includes hard 'G' (vulcanised rubber) and 'R' (sooty ragbag being ripped). Oatmeal 'N', noodle limp 'L' and the ivory backed hand mirror of 'O' take care of the whites.

I am puzzled by my French on which I see as the brimming tension surface of alcohol in a small glass.

Passing on to the blue group, there is steely 'X', thundercloud 'Z' and huckleberry 'K'. Since a subtle interaction exists between sound and shape, I see 'Q' as browner than 'K', while 'S' is not the light blue of 'C' but a curious mixture of azure and mother of pearl.

Adjacent tints do not merge, and diphthongs do not have sound colours of their own, numbers represented by a single character in some other language (thus the fluffy grey, three stemmed Russian letter that stands for 'SH'– a letter as old as the rushes of the Nile, influences its English representation).

…In the green group there are alder leaf 'F', the unripe apple of 'P' and pistachio 'T'. Dull green combined somehow with violet is the best I can do for 'W'.

The yellows comprise various 'E's' and 'I's', creamy bright-golden 'Y' and 'U', whose alphabetic value I can express only by 'brassy with an olive sheen.' In the brown group there are the rich rubbery tone of soft 'G', paler 'J' and the drab shoelace of 'H.'

Finally amongst the reds, 'B' has the tone called burnt sienna by painters, 'M' is a fold of pink flannel and I have at last perfectly matched 'V' with 'Rose Quartz' in Maerz and Paul's Dictionary of Colour. The word for rainbow, a primary but distinctly muddy rainbow, is in my private language the hardly pronounceable 'KZSPYGV'."

(Nabokov's mother Elena was a synaesthete, as was his wife Vera and his son Dmitri).

Mary Shelley
Two hundred years ago, five creative people were gathered in a house overlooking Lake Geneva in Switzerland. These included Mary Wollstonecraft Godwin, her lover and future husband, Percy Bysshe Shelley and Lord Byron. Mount Tambora in Indonesia had recently erupted – casting a spooky sky and unseasonably cool temperatures as far as Europe and North America. The group decided they would each write 'a story to wake the dead.'

Mary wrote the story of Dr Victor Frankenstein and the man-monster he created, telling the others the idea had come to her in a waking dream. It is said that the Gothic classic may have been inspired by the work of Conrad Dipple, a German alchemist who experimented on human bodies.

Mary gave Dr Frankenstein's monster synaesthesia: "It is with considerable difficulty that I remember the original era of my being; all the events of that period appear confused and indistinct. A strange multiplicity of sensations seized me, and I saw, felt, heard and smelt, at the same time, and it was, indeed, a long time before I learned to distinguish between the operations of my various senses." ('Frankenstein or the Modern Prometheus' Chapter 11 by Mary Shelley.

Frank Lloyd Wright
The famous architect claimed to hear music when he was designing buildings.

AN UNUSUAL CASE

Solomon Shereshevsky lived in Russia and was a newspaper reporter turned mnemonist discovered by neurophyschologist Aleksander Luria to have a very rare five-fold form of synaesthesia. Words and text were not only associated with highly vivid visual spatial imagery but also sound, taste, colour and sensation.

Shereshevsky aspired to be a violinist but became a journalist and then a professional mnemonist. He ended his career as a taxi driver in Moscow.

There were no limits to his memory. He never took notes during interviews. His editor sent him to Aleksander Luria for testing. He presented him with 70 digit matrices, complex scientific formulae and poems in foreign languages. He could memorise them in minutes.

He could recall things that happened in his crib. He could recount endless details of many things without form from lists of names to decades old conversations but he had difficulty grasping abstract concepts. The automatic and nearly permanent retention of every little detail due to synaesthesia greatly inhibited Shereshevsky from understanding much of what he read or heard.

When he heard a number he saw an image for that number. 'One is a proud well-built man, two is a high-spirited woman, three is a gloomy person and six is a man with a swollen foot.'

If he read when he was eating, he had a hard time understanding what he was reading. The taste of the food drowned out the sense. The sound of a word generated an image different from the word's meaning. It was a serious handicap as he couldn't block unwanted memories.

Aleksander Luria wrote 'The Mind of a Mnemonist' in 1968.

MY LIFE WITH SYNAESTHESIA

I have often been asked the question: "What difference do you think it has made to your life?" This is impossible to answer because it has always been part of me – like the green eyes I inherited from my father.

It is sometimes a difficult concept for some people to grasp – that the condition has nothing to do with imagination. The tastes I experience come from my brain not my mouth and there is absolutely nothing I can do about it. The tastes haven't changed over time – even though I may not have eaten the particular item for sixty years.

"Oh – it's memory then," some people say. Yes – the memory of the various tastes are probably hard-wired into my brain but I am doing nothing to consciously think about them and recall them. I have no control over it.

"You wouldn't have eaten a wide range of foods when you were a small child," argued another lady. That's true, I probably didn't. Some words evoke a very similar taste – but there are subtle differences. For instance, 'early' tastes of a square of milk chocolate sucked slowly. The name 'Margaret' also tastes of milk chocolate – but biting into a square rather than sucking it! 'Children' tastes of the way my Mum used to make rice pudding (without evaporated milk) and fairly milky. 'People' also tastes of rice pudding but drier - a little bit over-cooked.

I used to say odd things as a child (don't most of us!) which my mother considered to be imagination. Mostly, she told me not to be silly, when I said things like "I don't like the taste of that man." We had a neighbour called Eric – and I used to shy away from him. The name Eric tastes of ear-wax.

I was very fortunate to be read to a lot as a child – we shared a house at one stage with my Gran, Grandad, Aunt and Great Grandmother. I was surrounded by stories and words. I suffered a lot of illness as a child – tonsillitis and ear infections – which meant I got read to even more! I was also a poor eater – but this didn't become a problem until I started school at the age of four.

I was an early reader and can remember saying to the boy sitting next to me that I didn't like the taste of the word 'dog.'
"Do you like the taste of it?" I asked.
He gave me an odd look and said: "It's a book. It don't taste of anything."

I didn't agree – the word 'dog' definitely tasted of cold lamb, just as the word 'book' tasted of melting chocolate.

The boy's reaction was backed up by the teacher who told me:
"We're here to read words, not eat them."

I decided it was probably best to say nothing about the tastes that were piling into my brain as I read the words. However, it had a dramatic effect on my system. We did reading and writing in the morning at school – which meant that by lunchtime I was so full of word-tastes that I didn't want my school dinner.

I used to walk down to the school hall feeling sick when I smelled the school dinner. There would be a line of school dinner ladies clad in white overalls waiting to pile up our plates with stew, mashed potatoes and sponge pudding.

"I'm full up," I used to say – unable at that stage to differentiate between what I'd eaten and the words I'd read.

"You can't be – you haven't had anything," the dinner ladies used to say. I can remember one well-meaning one force-feeding me with cottage pie one day. (It didn't end well!)

My parents thought my lack of appetite was due to repeated bouts of tonsillitis. I did try to talk about the taste of words but nobody took any notice. If anything was said, it was a comment about my amazing imagination. As with school, I gave up mentioning it – although the situation didn't change.

I grew up in the 1950s and 1960s when interest in synaesthesia and knowledge about it had disappeared. People were locked in lunatic asylums for situations that would be unthinkable now – e.g. being homosexual. I knew of people who'd been locked up for having babies without being married and also a lady who'd dared to try and divorce her husband. The world was a different place then – the emphasis was on doing your best, fitting in and not drawing attention to yourself.

The tastes I experienced remained as vivid – I just got better at not mentioning anything about them.

When I was eighteen, I accepted a proposal of marriage. This wasn't the most sensible thing to have done – especially as we were poles apart where imagination and sensory perception were concerned. He also didn't approve of me writing, telling me to keep it quiet 'because people would think I was weird.'

After twenty-four years, the marriage came to an end and I was free to pursue the life I wanted. Immediately, the colours outside the window looked brighter. The grass shimmered and the daffodils shone like gold. I found new love and moved to a different town. I was forty-four when I met an artist and writer whose work I felt drawn to.

"Fridays are red," she said. "What colour are they to you?"
I replied that they didn't have a colour but they tasted of crisply fried fish fingers.
"I knew it," she said. "I could tell by your handwriting. I knew you were synaesthetic."
That was a watershed moment – the first time in my life that a name was given to the sensations I'd experienced.

For the first time in my life I felt I'd met someone who understood how I'd felt for so many years. It was a relief to feel that I didn't need to keep anything hidden any more. I read all I could find about synaesthesia and met more people who experienced various forms of it. I worked for a local charity organising creative writing workshops. Many of the people attending my workshops had mental health problems – a great many had synaesthesia, either inherited or acquired.

I feel very fortunate to have the gift of synaesthesia. The less I've had to hide it, the more effect it has on my life. The tastes I experience influence the names I give my characters and the words I use. I also experience vivid colours during dreams, head massage and meditation.

A SELECTION OF MY POEMS

Wishes

Most people don't notice
the sudden chill that strikes
as you pass the stag oak
at the corner of the field.

Hooked into technology
in a world of their own
they don't notice the crow's warning
from the top of the tree.

Stand still and listen with your heart
and you will hear
the rhythm of the earth
and the song of the flowers.

Stranger Danger

She was a girl who tasted of raspberry meringues.
When he first saw her – an orphan of the storm –
she looked at him with eyes that gleamed silver.
The black heart tattooed on her cheek
curved as she smiled showing teeth like polished rice.
He was lost for ever when she stretched out her hand
and led him into the dance.

Full Moon

A chill wind stirs the plum blossom
carries a scent of spices.

I gaze up at a full moon that pulsates towards me
from a star-filled sky.

Venus glows orange – a warning.

I remember last night's dream
of being lost in a tangerine mist.

The moon beams a spotlight pathway
lights up the gothic house ahead of me.
In a pool of water I see a face reflected
that is not mine.

The difference

I am an alien.

I am sure nobody else in this room
tastes
Marmite when they hear the word 'life'
or Plumrose tinned cream
when someone shouts the name 'Molly'
or strawberry jam when someone calls 'Robert.'

They are sound-tastes associated with childhood
and food I no longer eat but can still taste clearly
when I hear the words.

At school when learning to read
I said I didn't like the taste of the word 'complain.'
It conjured the taste of digestive biscuits –
too dry for a hot day in the classroom.

The teacher told me not to be silly.
We were here to read words not eat them.
By lunchtime I was too full of sounds to eat school dinner
and ended up standing in the corner for being wasteful.

Scientists now see my condition as something special.
I am a velvet clad laboratory rat.
I am a celebrity – I've been on the telly.
Watch out Big Brother.

ballet

ballet and map
tasted of McVitie's digestive biscuits –
chocolate for ballet – plain for map

in the dance studio edged with mirrors
and a wooden barre
I mapped my world in white satin steps

world tastes of pink blancmange
its jelly mould shape
encircled by crystalised violets
eaten in a sun-drenched garden

in the dance class I was pleased to be told
I had good elevation
even though the word had no taste

Stravaging

"Little girls who stravage get their north ears cut off
and eat stewed slugs for dinner."
I turn another somersault on the metal bar
at the end of the alley.
"You'll get appendicitis."
I think she says "a pen to write with"
which I'd like better than a pencil
so I do it again.

"Stop stravaging this minute. I want to get
to the shops today. And don't try and jump
that puddle. You'll splash your clean socks.
See, I knew you would."

I pick up a coin that somebody dropped and wait for her
to go on about coins being dirty
and you don't know who's touched them.

It's a farthing with a wren on it. Was the wren
stravaging too?

I move on a stage with my own excursion to the shops
walk on the wall by the Priory Gardens
and play hopscotch on the black and white stripes
of the zebra crossing with the lollipop beacons
that flash on off on off pid pod pid pod
like the beat of the metronome on my dancing teacher's piano.

Straggle

The other poets thought the word was negative
but to me it tasted
of evaporated milk and shortbread biscuits.

As a child I was used to "Hurry up. Stop scuffing your toes.
Don't straggle."

But the taste-map of the word
conjures up
feelings of safety
and pictures of gossamer fairies in the book
Mum read from every night
when I could rest in the velvet tunnel
of my imagination

Ragged

The rug in front of the roaring lion's tongue fire
is made of rags
spirals of colour positioned and tied
floppy as shoelaces.

The rag and bone man comes up the street
with his horse and cart and strange smelling cargo.
"Rag and bone. Rag and bone."
"Imagine being married to someone like that,"
says my Great Gran who isn't wearing her teeth.
"All rags and bones everywhere you looked."

He passes down the street
eyes predatory as a seagull's
and I think of the smell of damp newspapers
and how I wanted to know if they tasted of black jacks
like the word 'news' and was disappointed
to find they tasted of stale fish and dried mushrooms.

tastebuds

Jerusalem was red jelly not properly set
Venice tasted of white icing on a birthday cake
America was ground coffee
like the posh café in the High Street
Sweden was vegetable soup with dumplings
Finland was smoked haddock
and Antarctica was thick porridge
before you sprinkled brown sugar.

As a child, I mapped the world from the recipe book
inside my head.
At night I travelled by tastebud on the magic carpet
of my imagination.

fives

the pentagon has the power of the circle
and is the symbol of perfection

it is a combination of feminine number two
and masculine three

three symbolises meditation and religion

there are five senses
and five elements in Chinese astrology

my friend Jenny and I are synaesthetic –
something that affects one in 500,000 people

she sees five as the colour red
I taste crisply fried fish fingers

Jesus had five loaves and two fish to feed the five thousand

I wish on a five point star
that shines in my window
beside a silver sixpence moon

Quarantine

The word is raw cocoa with an after-taste of mint.
I experiment,
roll other words around my mouth

quaranta
querida
quarter
quarto

by the time I reach 'quart' the taste of cocoa disappears.

We were in quarantine, my brother and I,
pink with calamine lotion,
bickering under the orange satin bedspread
in Mum and Dad's ground floor bedroom shaded by the veranda
with a view of the garden we couldn't play in
because we had chicken pox and must stay in bed.

Quaranta
forty
school hymn practise
'forty days and forty nights
thou hast fasted in the wild'

and I wondered

did he have chicken pox too?

Grey school exercise books with a magical litany of measurements
on the back cover –

rod, perch, chain, furlong, acre
and the marzipan taste of inch.

MY GLOSSARY OF NAMES

Male

Alan	Lettuce with salad cream
Brian	Marmite sandwiches (white sliced bread)
Clive	Marmite
David	Oxtail soup
Eric	Earwax
George	Yorkshire pudding
James	Jammy dodger biscuits
John	Crusty white bread and butter
Mark	Skin on sausages
Martin	Tinned tomatoes
Michael	Evaporated milk
Paul	Hard boiled eggs
Peter	Tinned marrowfat peas
Richard	Rice pudding (evaporated milk)
Robert	Strawberry jam – Gran's home made
Stephen	Biting on silver paper
William	Thick porridge – no sugar

<u>Female</u>

Alice	Lettuce – (my grandfather's)
Alicia	Tablets with rubbery coating
Angela	Blackcurrant jelly
Ann/Anne	Skin on Granny Smith apple
Barbara	Rhubarb (cooked)
Christine	Crispbread – no butter
Catherine	plain steamed pudding
Cathy	coffee made with milk
Carol	Plain cake
Caroline	Sultana cake
Elizabeth	Heinz tomato soup
Emily	Semolina
Grace	Fat on cold lamb
Hannah	Sultana cake
Helen	Cucumber
Hilary	Rhubarb
Joan	Toe nails
Joyce	Cocktail cherries
Lorna	Apple cake

Lucy	Golden syrup
Margaret	Milk chocolate – from the fridge
Mary	Whipped double cream
Molly	Plumrose tinned cream
Paula	Apple sponge
Sarah	whipped double cream
Vera	Vanilla ice cream - homemade
Vicki	Thick porridge with brown sugar

MY GLOSSARY OF WORDS

(This is just an extract – there are many more!)

ballet	chocolate digestives
bank	baked beans
chess	after-taste of roasted chestnuts
children	rice pudding – made without evaporated milk
early	milk chocolate sucked slowly
engagement	greengage jam
fact	pork crackling/crisp fat on a pork chop
feather	whipped cream
Friday	crisply fried fish fingers
God	roast lamb
hospital	over-ripe banana
interesting	cabbage/spinach
garden	boiled new potatoes
jealous	the jelly-stuff on a pork pie
late	dark chocolate – sucked slowly
life	Marmite
map	digestive biscuits

maths	stale digestive biscuits
money	baked beans
morning	Cornflakes + top of the milk
music	vanilla ice cream
object/objection	apricot jam
peace	unripe banana
people	rice pudding - overcooked
punish	liquorice
punishment	liquorice with an after-taste of mint
rich	rice pudding with evaporated milk
school	evaporated milk
secret	milk chocolate – sucked slowly
spider	Marmite
surprise	strawberry cream chocolate
Thursday	coffee made with milk – skin forming
time	KitKat (milk chocolate)
work	boiled potatoes
world	pink blancmange

TASTE MAP OF PLACES

(this is an extract of places and tastes – there are many more)

America	the smell/taste of ground coffee
Antarctica	thick porridge made with milk
China	rice pudding + skin – made with ordinary milk
Cornwall	the crumble bit of an apple crumble
Dorset	baked apple with brown sugar
Egypt	rice pudding – evaporated milk + nutmeg
India	the smell/taste of powdery tea at the bottom of the box
Persia	sherbet
Sweden	vegetable soup with dumplings
Venice	white icing on a birthday cake

FURTHER READING

'The Man Who Tasted Shapes' by Richard E Cytowic (pub 1993 MIT Press)

'Wednesday Is Indigo Blue: discovering the brain of synaesthesia' by Richard E Cytowic and David Eagleman (pub 2009 MIT Press)

'Synaesthesia – the strangest thing' by John Harrison (pub 2001Oxford University Press)

'Tasting the Universe: people who see colours in words and rainbows in symphonies' by Maureen Seaberg (pub 2011 New Page Books)

'Synesthetes – a handbook' by Sean A Day (pub 2016 Create Space)

'A Natural History of the Senses' by Diane Ackerman (pub 1990 Random House)

'The Frog Who Croaked Blue: synaesthesia and the mixing of the senses' by Jamie Ward
(pub 2008 Routledge)

'The Mind of a Mnemonist: a little book about a vast memory' by Alexander Luria (pub 1968 Basic Books Inc USA)

'Blue Cats & Chartreuse Kittens – how synesthetes color their worlds' by Patricia Lynne Duffy (pub 2001 Henry Holt)

WEBSITES

UK Synaestheia Association
www.uksynaesthesia.com

American Synesthesia Association
www.synesthesia.info

Sounding Art -Jane Mackay
www.soundingart.com

Synaesthesia Network
www.thesynaesthesianetwork.com

Painting Music – Phillip Schreibman
www.paintingmusic.com

James Wannerton - blog
www.tastethetube.com/blogs/james-wannerton

The Synesthesia Battery
www.synesthesia.org

Sean A Day - The Synesthesia List
www.daysyn.com

ABOUT THE AUTHOR

Sue Johnson is a poet, short story writer and novelist. She is a Writing Magazine Creative Writing Tutor and also runs her own brand of writing workshops.

Sue has a passion for history and a keen interest in mental health. Her other interests include walking, reading, yoga, cooking and learning languages.

For further details of Sue's courses, workshops and critique service, see her website
www.writers-toolkit.co.uk

Follow her on Twitter @SueJohnson9

OTHER BOOKS BY SUE JOHNSON

POETRY
Tasting Words, Hearing Colours
Curious Women
Tales of Trees (with Bob Woodroofe)
Journey (with Bob Woodroofe)
The Evesham Café Collection (with Angela Fitch)

NOVELS
Fable's Fortune
The Yellow Silk Dress
Fortune's Promise
Apple Orchard, Lemon Grove

NOVELLA
A Solstice Tale

SHORT STORIES
Time To Put Your Feet Up

NON-FICTION
Creative Alchemy: 12 steps from inspiration to finished novel
Surfing the Rainbow: visualization and chakra balancing for writers
Writing Success: poetry, flash fiction & short story exercises

See Sue's website for details of her writing courses, talks and
critique service
www.writers-toolkit.co.uk

TOADSTONE PRESS

Printed in Great Britain
by Amazon